AUG 1 6 2005

xBiog Frank.B Strei.T
Streissguth, Thomas, 1958-
Benjamin Franklin

JUN

Benjamin Franklin

Tom Streissguth

In Consultation with Martha Cosgrove, M.A. and Reading Specialist

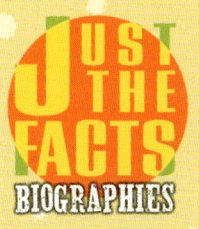

Just the Facts
BIOGRAPHIES

◢ Lerner Publications Company/Minneapolis

Martha Cosgrove has a master's degree from the University of Minnesota in secondary education, with an emphasis on developmental and remedial reading. She is licensed in 7–12 English and language arts, developmental reading, and remedial reading. She has had several works published, and she gives numerous state and national presentations in her areas of expertise.

Copyright © 2005 by Tom Streissguth

All rights reserved. International copyright secured. No part of this book may be reproduced, stored in a retrieval system, or transmitted in any form or by any means—electronic, mechanical, photocopying, recording, or otherwise—without the prior written permission of Lerner Publications Company, except for the inclusion of brief quotations in an acknowledged review.

Lerner Publications Company
A division of Lerner Publishing Group
241 First Avenue North
Minneapolis, MN U.S.A.

Website address: www.lernerbooks.com

Library of Congress Cataloging-in-Publication Data

Streissguth, Thomas, 1958–
　Benjamin Franklin / by Tom Streissguth.
　　p. cm. – (Just the facts bios)
　Includes bibliographical references and index.
　Contents: The famous Doctor Franklin—Making his fortune—Franklin of Philadelphia—A mission in Britain—More trouble in the Colonies—Shots heard 'round the world—Working for a new nation—A last journey home.
　　ISBN: 0-8225-2210-1 (lib. bdg. : alk. paper)
　1. Franklin, Benjamin, 1706-1790–Juvenile literature. 2. Statesmen–United States–Biography–Juvenile literature. 3. Scientists–United States–Biography–Juvenile literature. 4. Inventors–United States–Biography–Juvenile literature. 5. Printers–United States–Biography–Juvenile literature. [1. Franklin, Benjamin, 1706-1790. 2. Statesmen. 3. Scientists. 4. Inventors. 5. Printers.] I. Title. II. Series.
E302.6.F8S915 2005
973.3'092–dc22   2003027284

Manufactured in the United States of America
1 2 3 4 5 6 – JR – 10 09 08 07 06 05

Contents

1. The Famous Doctor Franklin 4
2. Making His Fortune 24
3. Franklin of Philadelphia 41
4. A Mission in Britain 59
5. More Trouble in the Colonies 69
6. Shots Heard 'Round the World ... 77
7. Working for a New Nation 87
8. A Last Journey Home 99
   Glossary 106
   Source Notes 108
   Selected Bibliography 109
   Further Reading and Websites 110
   Index 111

CHAPTER 1
THE FAMOUS DOCTOR FRANKLIN

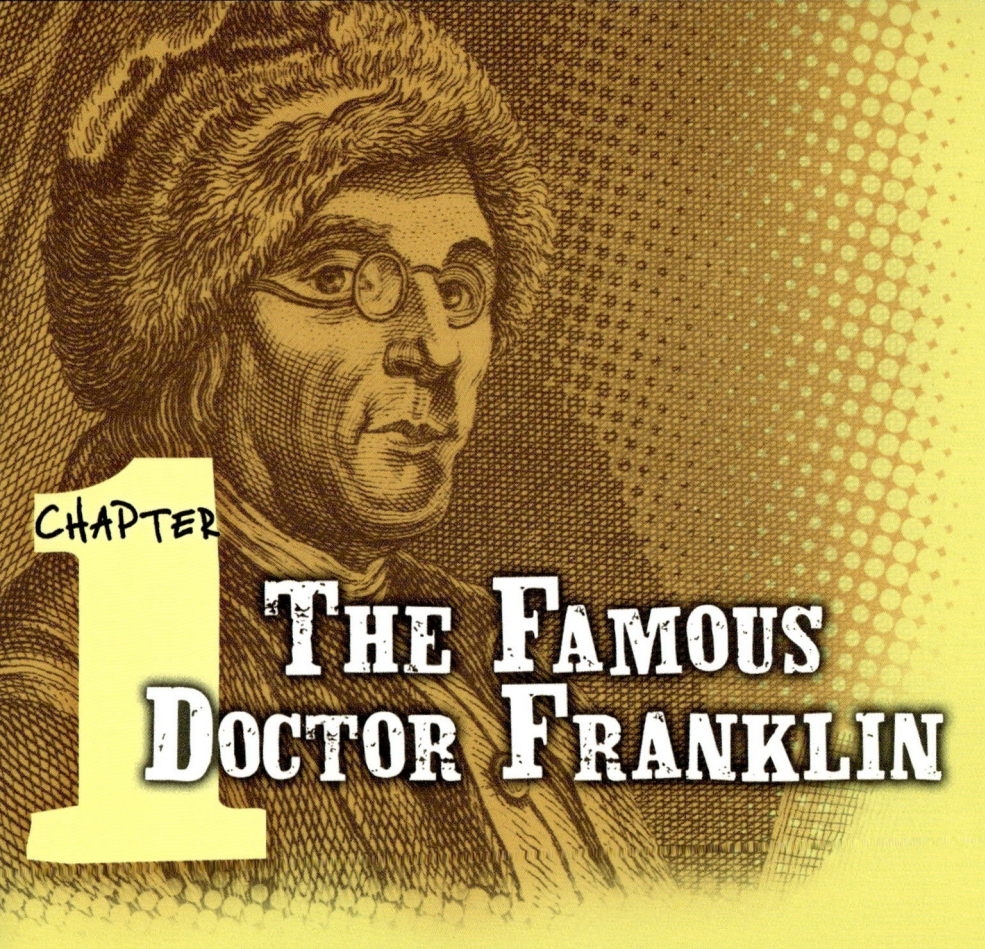

(Above) Benjamin Franklin wore a raccoon skin hat when he was in France.

IN FEBRUARY OF 1778, a man arrived in a horse-drawn coach at a set of big iron gates. He was visiting Versailles, the grand palace of Louis XVI, the king of France. The man was seventy-two years old and a bit overweight. His age and weight forced him to move slowly. He passed the guards and was taken down a long hall to a room. There, members of the royal court were waiting for the king.

The members of the court dressed in stylish white wigs and colorful clothes. The men wore coats with lace and gold trim. The women wore fancy silk dresses that swept across the floor. But the heavy-set visitor's clothes were simple. He wore a plain, brown velvet coat. He'd brought a wig but didn't like the way it fit, so he decided not to wear it. Instead, he wore a cap made from raccoon skin. He'd brought it from the British colonies in North America, where he lived. His face was rounded. His forehead was high. Behind his glasses, his eyes were alert and cool.

Then King Louis appeared. He looked the most magnificent of all, as a king should. His sword glittered. So did the priceless gems on his white fur robe. Everyone made a deep bow. The old man bowed as well. He politely removed his cap.

The old man was Benjamin Franklin. The French deeply respected Franklin. They called him Doctor Franklin. He was famous for his knowledge of science. People all over the world had heard about his experiments with electricity and especially with lightning.

But Franklin wasn't visiting the court as a scientist. He was visiting as an ambassador—the person chosen by American leaders to talk to the French leaders. The Americans had begun a revolt.

6　Benjamin Franklin

Louis XVI of France

They were trying to break away from the rule of Great Britain. They sent Franklin to France to ask for money and supplies.

Franklin had been living in a house between Versailles and Paris, the French capital. He had met many important people and had asked them to help the Americans. He had also been trying to convince the French to sign two treaties, or agreements. The treaties would have put France officially on the side of the Americans against the British. France and Great Britain had long been enemies. Both countries had tried to control North America by building forts and creating colonies there. After many years of war, the British controlled most of the continent.

The French called North America the "New World." They thought of it as wild and pure. Maybe Franklin dressed so simply that day to remind the French that he came from this pure land. One important Frenchman wrote that Franklin was "simple but dignified." He said that it seemed like the rough and straightforward Franklin had been "brought by magic" into their delicate world.

The same man wrote that the French loved the idea of liberty, or freedom. And Franklin reminded them of liberty. John Adams, another American working for liberty, also visited France. He noticed that almost everyone thought of Franklin as "a friend to human kind." Franklin himself wrote that most of the French believed the American fight was a fight for all people. He wrote that the French believed "we are fighting for their Liberty in defending our own."

If the Americans won their war, they would begin a democracy. That meant they would elect their leaders from their own people. They would no longer be ruled by the British king, George III. Maybe Louis XVI wondered whether other kings, such as himself, might be threatened if the Americans succeeded. He must have worried whether France could afford the cost of America's risky war. Still, largely because of Franklin, Louis signed the treaties on February 6, 1778. It was a major victory for the American colonists.

Benjamin Franklin had done his job. With the help of France, the American revolt would succeed. The colonies would be free from the cruel and unfair rule of the British. But Franklin had once been very loyal to the British king. His earlier life held no sign that he would be such an important part of a revolt or be very important at all. He came from a humble working family—the Franklins of Ecton, a town in northern Great Britain.

From the Old World to the New

The Franklins had lived in Ecton for many generations. The law in Great Britain required all citizens to stay in their country. But after the discovery of the New World, Britain's leaders encouraged citizens to go to North America. With more people in the new lands, Britain could set up colonies. The colonists could send lumber, furs, tobacco, silver, and gold back to Great Britain.

In 1683 Benjamin's father, Josiah Franklin, took his family to the New World. He and his wife, Anne, and their three children landed in Boston. This busy city was in the Massachusetts Bay Colony. Boston was a port—a city with an important harbor where ships could land and people could trade goods. In Britain, Josiah had been a dyer of fabrics. But in Boston, there was not much need for dyers. So Josiah became a chandler. A chandler made candles and soap.

Boston's port was a busy place during Franklin's early life.

10 Benjamin Franklin

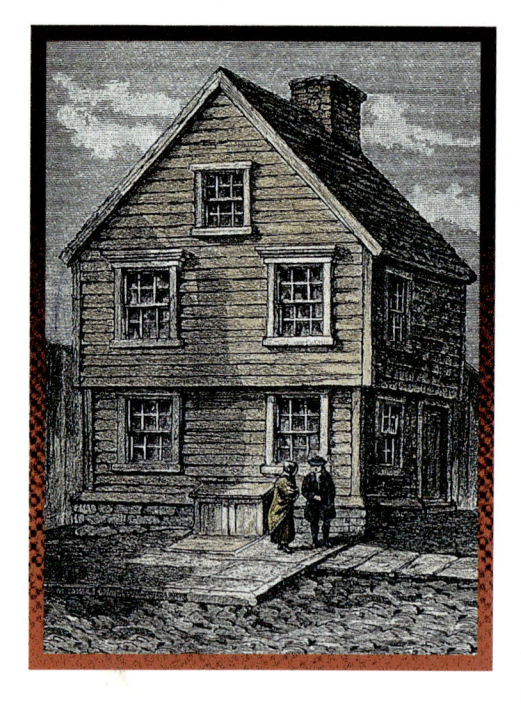

This illustration shows Benjamin Franklin's birthplace in Boston.

In 1688 Anne Franklin died after giving birth to her seventh child. Josiah then took a second wife, Abiah Folger. Their eighth child (Josiah's tenth boy) was born on January 17, 1706. They named him Benjamin after Josiah's brother, a very religious Christian man. In all, Abiah gave birth to ten children.

The family crowded into a small house. Many of Josiah's children from his first marriage joined them. The house was warmed with fireplaces and lit by candles. It must have bustled with people and activity. Soon, Josiah became a respected person in the city. Many people, including Boston's leaders,

The Famous Doctor Franklin

came to the house to get his advice. And Josiah always seemed to have guests for dinner. According to Benjamin, Josiah thought lively, adult conversation would "improve the minds of his children."

Benjamin loved to run in the streets of Boston and to swim in the Charles River that flowed through the city. One day, Benjamin led a group of boys in stealing some stone. The stone was to be used to build a new house. But the boys used it to build a small dock in a nearby swamp. From their dock, they caught small fish called minnows. When the theft and the thieves were discovered, the parents of all the boys were very angry. Benjamin's father told him that he should always be honest.

Another time, Benjamin decided that swimming in the ordinary way wasn't good enough. So he built a set of wooden paddles (like modern fins) to help him swim faster. He also tied himself to a kite so that it could help to pull him across the river. Even as a boy, Benjamin learned by closely watching the world around him.

> **IT'S A FACT!**
> Benjamin Franklin is the only Founding Father to be elected to the International Swimming Hall of Fame.

Even though Benjamin often caused trouble, his father was proud of his son's curiosity and intelligence. When Benjamin was eight, Josiah enrolled him in Boston Grammar School. It taught subjects such as the Latin language that helped boys prepare for professional careers. At this time, parents most often chose what their children would do as their life's work. And so it was for the Franklins. Josiah's other sons were learning ordinary jobs. But Josiah wanted Benjamin to become a minister. But Benjamin was restless and did not work hard in school. Josiah took him out of the school after just one year.

Josiah next enrolled Benjamin in a different school. And he began to reconsider Benjamin's future. To become a minister, Benjamin would soon have to go to college. But Josiah could not afford to pay for college. Besides, Benjamin didn't seem like a minister. He didn't have strong faith, like his Uncle Benjamin. Instead, he seemed to question everything. Josiah withdrew Benjamin from the second school. Benjamin had received one more year of education.

Boston was then the largest town in North America. Nearly twelve thousand people lived there. Sailing ships brought goods from Europe, the

The Famous Doctor Franklin 13

West Indies, and Africa into its harbor. Ship captains traded for local products such as timber, fish, and rum. They could then sell these products in Great Britain. A person would always find plenty of customers for soap and candles in a town like Boston. Josiah decided Benjamin would join him in his own workshop, learning the trade of chandler.

Learning a Trade

Ten-year-old Benjamin helped to make candles from wicks and tallow (melted animal fat). He also helped make soap by boiling tallow with wood ashes in a cast-iron kettle. The work was hot, dirty, and boring. Benjamin knew he didn't want to follow in his father's footsteps.

From about 1716 to 1718, young Benjamin worked with his father as a chandler making candles and soap.

Josiah realized that being a chandler would never satisfy Benjamin. He took his son walking around town to watch bricklayers, carpenters, and other workers at their tasks. But none of these jobs interested Benjamin. Benjamin loved to read, so Josiah finally decided that he might like to work as a printer.

In 1718 Josiah sent Benjamin to his older brother James, who owned a nearby printing shop. Benjamin was to become James's apprentice, or student-worker. This meant signing an indenture, an agreement that made a young worker stay with a master, or teacher, for a set period. When Benjamin signed his indenture, he was only twelve years old. The indenture said he would work for James for nine years, until Benjamin turned twenty-one. In the last year of the indenture, Benjamin would earn money, but not before.

James showed his brother how to make letters, or type, from melted lead. He taught Benjamin how to set the type in wooden printing molds. Benjamin also worked the printing press. This was a big wooden machine that pressed sheets of paper against the ink-coated type. Using this process, Benjamin and James could print posters, pamphlets,

The Famous Doctor Franklin 15

Benjamin preferred printing to candle making.

newspapers, and even books.

Benjamin liked his job as a printer. He loved working with words. He often read for hours at a time, well into the night. Whenever he came across a new book, he read it. He wanted to know what the writer had to say. Benjamin also discovered new worlds by reading newspapers and pamphlets. He enjoyed the lively arguments over politics, religion, and science that writers in Boston carried on.

In November of 1718, Benjamin wrote a poem called *The Lighthouse Tragedy*. It was based on the true story of the death of a lighthouse keeper and his family. Benjamin knew his poem was not great,

Benjamin Franklin sells his ballad *The Lighthouse Tragedy* in the streets of Boston.

but he thought he could sell copies of it. His brother agreed to print it. Then Benjamin took the copies out into the streets. He sold them to people who passed by for a few pennies each. Benjamin was thrilled, but his father did not approve. He said that "verse-makers" were usually beggars. Benjamin should learn useful skills and earn his money. That was more important than poetry.

The hardest part of Benjamin's life was getting along with James. "Thou' a Brother," wrote

Benjamin, "he considered himself as my Master, & me as his Apprentice." James treated Benjamin as an apprentice and not as a brother. He could be mean to Benjamin. Sometimes the brothers took their arguments to their father, who usually took Benjamin's side.

In 1721 James Franklin started his own newspaper, the *New England Courant*. Publishing a newspaper was even more interesting than printing books. Each day there were unusual events or exciting arguments. Newspapers carried opinions about all of them. Day after day, readers bought newspapers to read the latest lively essays.

Fifteen-year-old Benjamin wanted to write for the *Courant,* but his brother would not let him. James thought Benjamin was too young. He didn't think Benjamin knew enough about the world to write the kinds of articles James needed. Benjamin decided to write an article and sign it with a made-up name. Late one night, he slipped the article under the front door of his brother's shop. He had signed it "Silence Do-good." Newspaper writers at this time often used pen names like this. James was not surprised to find an article signed with a pen name. James liked the article enough to print it. In

18 Benjamin Franklin

fact, he even advertised in the *Courant,* asking the writer to send more articles to him. So Benjamin sent in more. He wrote many articles as Silence Do-good and under other names.

Benjamin was sometimes ashamed that he had so little education. So he tried to educate himself. He bought any book he could afford. He borrowed books when he couldn't buy them. He studied many subjects, including math and religion. He worked to improve his writing. He studied articles by good writers and copied their style.

Benjamin Franklin studied hard to educate himself.

The Famous Doctor Franklin 19

THE AUTOBIOGRAPHY OF BENJAMIN FRANKLIN

Many quotes in this book come from Benjamin Franklin's autobiography. He began writing about his life as a way of telling his son, William, about himself. He continued when others told him that many young people could benefit from the lessons of his life. The autobiography covers the years up to 1757. In the following section, Franklin has become a vegetarian and cooks for himself instead of eating with the workers from his brother's printing shop. At that time, people spelled words in lots of ways. There weren't strict rules, so some of the words in the autobiography look different than they would in modern times.

> When about 16 Years of Age, I happen'd to meet with a Book written by one Tyron, recommending a Vegetable Diet. I determined to go into it.... I made my self acquainted with Tyron's Manner of preparing some of his Dishes, such as Boiling Potatoes, or Rice, making Hasty Pudding, & a few others, and then propos'd to my Brother, that if he would give me Weekly half the Money he paid for my Board [food], I would board my self. He instantly agreed to it, and I presently found that I could save half what he paid me. This was an additional Fund for buying Books.

One time, Josiah read a letter Benjamin had written to a friend. The two young men had been disagreeing about whether girls should get the same education as boys. (At this time, only boys studied academic subjects such as math and reading.) Benjamin's letter argued for better schooling for girls. Josiah did not comment on the topic, but he did show Benjamin ways to make his points more effectively.

Benjamin took his father's advice. He believed that his father's coaching helped him become a better writer.

BREAKING FREE

James and Benjamin soon found that the newspaper business had risks. The leaders of Massachusetts Bay Colony, including Boston, were Puritans. Their religion gave them a strict sense of duty, which included making local society follow their beliefs. They expected citizens to obey Puritan leadership. They did not allow much criticism.

Sometimes James Franklin published articles that seemed disrespectful of these leaders. Other articles questioned them. At first, the leaders did nothing. But after a while, they grew angry. One day, James published an article making fun of them for being slow to capture some pirates. After that, the leaders acted quickly. In 1722 the Governor's Council of Massachusetts sentenced James to one month in prison. They also told him he could no longer publish a newspaper.

The *Courant* could continue, however, if the editor wasn't James. So James asked Benjamin to become its editor. James knew that the Puritan leaders might think his apprentice was pretending

The Famous Doctor Franklin

to be editor while James was still in charge. So James released Benjamin from his indenture and made sure everyone knew about it. Then he and Benjamin signed a new indenture and kept it secret.

Meanwhile, James was still strict and was sometimes violent with Benjamin. "Perhaps I was too saucy & provoking," Benjamin wrote. More likely he was too stubborn and proud to take his brother's treatment. The public thought that Benjamin was no longer indentured to James. So Benjamin took advantage of this fact and announced he was quitting.

James was angry and asked all the other printers in Boston not to hire Benjamin. This made it difficult for Benjamin to earn a living in his hometown. He decided to leave Boston. But he knew his father would not let him go. "If I attempted to go openly," Benjamin wrote, "Means would be used to prevent me."

In September of 1723, at the age of seventeen, Benjamin sailed on a ship to New York. In New York, he was three hundred miles from home and had "very little Money in my Pocket." He knew no one in the city, and he found no work. So he went on to Perth Amboy, a settlement on the coast of

Franklin walks along a Philadelphia street, as a young woman watches. He later learned that her name was Deborah Read.

New Jersey. Then he walked to Burlington, a town on the Delaware River. From there, he boarded a riverboat bound for Philadelphia, a port city in the colony of Pennsylvania.

Benjamin reached Philadelphia dirty, hungry, and exhausted. With some of his few remaining coins, he bought some rolls of bread. As he made his way through the busy city, he paid close attention to everything he saw and heard. One sight stayed with him for a long time. It was the sight of a young woman standing in a doorway. She saw him too. He later wrote that she "thought I made, as I certainly did, a most awkward, ridiculous appearance." Benjamin did not talk to her. But he would soon find out that her name was Deborah Read.

Benjamin found a small building where some religious people called Quakers were meeting. He went inside. There, the seventeen-year-old runaway dropped into an uncomfortable pew and quickly fell asleep.

Chapter 2
Making His Fortune

Young Benjamin Franklin awoke a few hours later. He asked advice about where to stay and soon found a room. It was in the home of John Read, the father of Deborah Read. Then Franklin started looking for work. Within a few days, he had a job with a printer named Samuel Keimer. Franklin was grateful for the work. But his employer had little skill with a printing press. Franklin thought about starting a shop of his own. At this time, though, most printing supplies and equipment came from Great Britain. He did not have the money for that.

Franklin's brother-in-law, Robert Homes, was concerned over Franklin's leaving Boston. So Franklin wrote a letter to Homes explaining his good reasons for leaving. Homes, a ship's captain, showed the letter to Sir William Keith. Keith was governor of

Sir William Keith visited the printing shop where Franklin worked.

Pennsylvania. He was impressed and called Franklin "a young Man of promising Parts." He also said the printers in Philadelphia were all "wretched." He was sure Franklin could do a better job.

One day, Keith stopped by Keimer's shop and asked for Franklin. Keimer was stunned by the governor's visit. He stared "like a Pig poison'd," according to Franklin. Keith took Franklin to a nearby tavern to talk. He talked the young man into traveling back to Boston. Keith encouraged Franklin to ask his father for a business loan. He even gave Franklin a letter supporting the idea.

Franklin returned to Boston looking like he was doing well. He wore a watch and a fine new suit. These were signs of success in a time when clothes were expensive. Josiah Franklin listened to his son and read Keith's letter. But he did not give Franklin a loan. Instead, he told the seventeen-year-old to work hard and save his money until he was twenty-one. If he had almost enough money by then, his father would lend him the rest.

Franklin returned to Sir William Keith in Philadelphia. "Since he will not set you up," Keith told Franklin, "I will do it my self." Keith did not mean he would loan Franklin the money himself. He meant he would recommend Franklin to wealthy friends in London, the capital of Great Britain. Franklin had only to go there. He could obtain loans and buy the equipment. In exchange for Keith's help, Franklin would then help Keith. Back in Philadelphia, he would print pamphlets and perhaps a newspaper supporting Keith.

During these months, Franklin and Deborah Read had grown close. "I had a great Respect & Affection for her," Franklin later wrote. And he "had some Reason to believe she had the same for me." The two young people talked about getting married. But Deborah's mother advised them to wait. Franklin would be leaving for London soon. And besides, as Franklin pointed out, "We both

Making His Fortune   27

A portrait of Franklin as a young man

were very young, only a little above 18."

Franklin was also too poor to take a wife. So he and Deborah exchanged "some promises," as Franklin wrote. Then he sailed away from Philadelphia on November 5, 1724. On board the ship was a friend of Keith's. He was carrying a bag of letters from the governor and others. Keith had promised that letters recommending Franklin were included in the bag.

Seven weeks later, on Christmas Eve, the ship docked in London. Keith's friend and Franklin looked in the mailbag. But Franklin's letters were not there. Franklin was upset. "What shall we think of a Governor's playing such pitiful Tricks... on a poor ignorant Boy!" he said.

He was thousands of miles from home in one of the biggest cities in the world. On board the ship, he had met Thomas Denham, a merchant trader from Philadelphia. He turned to Denham for advice. Denham told Franklin that Keith would never send the letters. He said Franklin could improve his skills by getting a job with one of the expert printers of London.

Franklin liked the idea of staying in London. People from all over the world lived in the huge city. It fascinated him. He quickly found work at a printing house. He wrote pamphlets on topics that interested him. He and Denham became friends and explored the great city together. They visited its churches and roamed its streets. Franklin met many writers, scientists, and others in London restaurants and taverns. Months slipped by. Franklin wrote only once to Deborah Read. He said he was "not likely to return soon."

Denham and Franklin eventually made a business deal. Franklin would work in Denham's

> **IT'S A FACT!**
> While in London this first time, Franklin was offered a job giving swimming lessons. He stuck with printing.

London was a bustling port city when Franklin visited.

business in Philadelphia. He would take care of Denham's store and keep the accounting books. Franklin would be able to learn the business of merchant trading. Denham said he would then loan Franklin money so he could make his own trading voyages. Franklin might eventually become a rich man. It was an excellent opportunity for Franklin. On July 22, 1726, he sailed back to Britain's colonies in North America.

On the voyage home, Franklin made a list of twelve virtues. Virtues are qualities or traits of goodness. Franklin wanted to behave virtuously. That meant working hard, telling the truth, saving his money, and speaking ill of no one. He noted his successes and failures each day on a chart divided into days of the week. He was so proud of his successes that he had to add a thirteenth virtue to practice: humility (not being overly proud of himself).

A Profitable Debate

Franklin had been away from Philadelphia for more than a year and a half. He quickly renewed old friendships. And he walked the streets where he had once been hungry and tired.

While he was gone, Deborah Read had changed. She had married a potter, John Rogers. Rogers had then disappeared. Franklin felt sorry for Deborah. To him, she seemed "generally dejected, seldom chearful, and avoided company."

Early in 1727, Denham died. His business closed, and Franklin went back to work for Samuel Keimer. In London, Franklin had worked for some of the best printers and journalists in the world. He was a masterful printer, much better than Keimer, he thought. The two argued often. Finally, Keimer fired him.

Then Keimer won a contract to print paper money for the colony of New Jersey. The job involved uncommon skills such as the detailed engraving of copper plates. Keimer needed Franklin. He asked Franklin to work in his shop in Burlington, New Jersey. Franklin would become an expert at printing money. And he knew that would lead to more work in the future. He took the job.

Making His Fortune   31

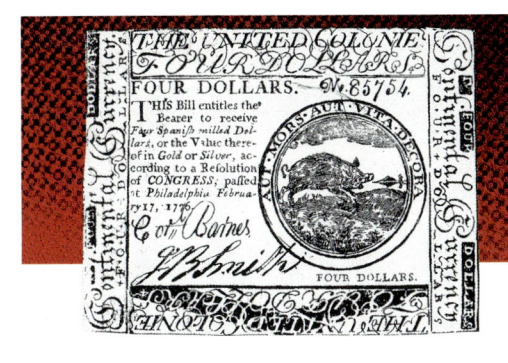

Franklin first printed paper money for the British colonies *(left)*. He would later print money during the American Revolution.

In Burlington, Franklin made a new friend. Hugh Meredith was one of Keimer's apprentices. Before long, Hugh's father suggested that the two young men go into business together. Mr. Meredith advanced them some money. With it, Franklin and Hugh Meredith secretly ordered printing equipment and supplies. Franklin and Meredith resigned from Keimer's shop soon after the New Jersey money was completed. Then they set up a business of their own in Philadelphia.

Some people didn't think paper money was a good idea. Most rich people kept their savings in gold and silver coin. Many feared their metal money would lose value if Pennsylvania issued paper money. Many other people, such as small merchants and workers, disagreed. They thought paper money would help the colony's economy grow, because money would be more available to buy things.

Franklin was on the side of paper money. To promote his views, he wrote and printed a pamphlet. It was called *A Modest Enquiry into the Nature and Necessity of a Paper-Currency*. Then he distributed it for free. His arguments helped convince the members of the Pennsylvania Assembly (who made the colony's laws). They voted to issue paper money. Franklin got the contract for printing it. This was "a very profitable Jobb and a great help to me," he wrote.

Franklin met many people, and he was very skilled at what he did. For these reasons, he continued to get contracts. He had contracts to print new laws, speeches, and assembly proceedings. He wrote, "After getting the first hundred [dollars], it is more easy to get the second."

Eventually, Franklin was appointed official printer for the Pennsylvania government. Soon after, he got the same jobs for the governments of New Jersey and Delaware. The money he earned helped him pay off the debts of his new business. And people realized he had been right about paper money.

THE PENNSYLVANIA GAZETTE

At that time, Philadelphia had only one newspaper. It was the *American Weekly Mercury*. Its owner and

By Franklin's time, Philadelphia was the biggest city in the American colonies.

editor was Andrew Bradford. Bradford was also the colony's postmaster. As postmaster, Bradford had several advantages. He could have his paper delivered for free with other mail. Also, he was the first person to receive news from Europe. So he could include articles based on the latest European news in his newspaper. Colonists were very interested in European events. This led more colonists to buy his paper.

Still, Franklin believed there was room for another newspaper in this growing city. He decided to start one. Unfortunately, Samuel Keimer heard about Franklin's plan. He was still angry with Franklin for quitting. Keimer decided to start a newspaper of his own. The first edition came out in

December of 1728. But it was small, just a single sheet, with little news of interest.

Franklin began writing articles for Bradford's paper. In them, he made fun of Keimer's paper. Many people read the articles. They began to see Keimer's paper as worthless. Keimer became frustrated and sold the paper. His buyers were Benjamin Franklin and Hugh Meredith.

Meredith quit the business within a year to start a farm. Franklin borrowed enough money to buy him out. By this time, Franklin had changed the content of *The Pennsylvania Gazette*. Besides news, it contained articles on the many things that interested him. He wrote about the weather, the circulation of the blood, and the causes of earthquakes. Franklin's Gazette was well written and expertly printed. It was sold all over the city and in some neighboring towns. Franklin made money from selling copies. Businesses paid him to advertise their stores in the paper.

In the meantime, Franklin and Deborah Read had revived the "mutual affection" they shared. "But there were great objections to our union," Franklin wrote. Deborah's husband, John Rogers, might still be alive. If so, then Deborah was a

Franklin was relieved to find that Deborah still cared for him even after their years apart.

married woman. Also, Rogers owed many people money. Any new husband of Deborah's might be asked to pay these debts.

Another problem was the fact that Benjamin Franklin had a son without having married the boy's mother. Most Puritans looked down on this sort of behavior. Historians do not know who the mother was. And they do not know exactly when William Franklin was born. Most likely it was sometime in 1729 or 1730.

On September 1, 1730, Franklin married Deborah. He was twenty-four years old. He and Deborah moved into a new home at 139 Market Street. Little William also joined their household. The printing shop and the offices of the *Gazette* were on the first floor of the house. From a small

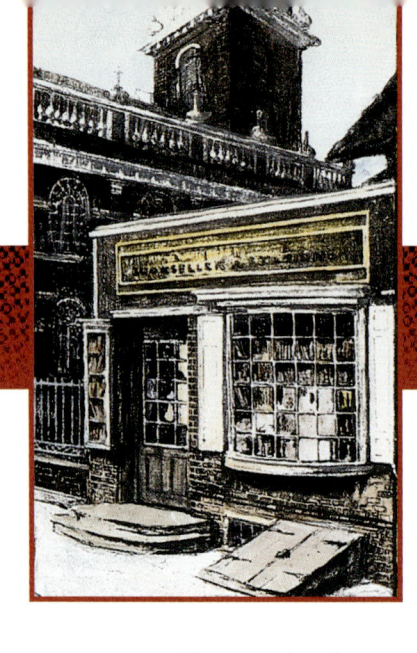

Deborah Franklin and her mother helped Ben run Franklin's shop.

shop next door, the Franklins sold books and pamphlets. They also sold paper, ink, soap, candles, tea, coffee, and other items. In addition, Franklin often lent money to his customers. So the shop also served as a small, private bank.

"Debby," as Franklin sometimes called his wife, "prov'd a good & faithful Helpmate." The two tried "to make each other happy." Two years later, Deborah gave birth to a son, Francis Franklin. They nicknamed him "Franky." The Franklins had become a family of four.

POOR RICHARD

Franklin knew that the public was often hard to please. No one could tell whether a book would sell many copies. Franklin did not take many risks. He looked for safe investments.

He found one in the form of an almanac. An almanac is a collection of facts that appears in a

Making His Fortune 37

new edition every year. In Franklin's time, almanacs listed the time of sunrise each day and predicted the weather. They suggested the best days to plant and harvest crops. Almanacs contained a lot of useful information. Nearly every colonial family owned one.

Franklin began publishing his own almanac in 1732. As he had done in the past, he used a pen name. He called himself "Richard Saunders," or "Poor Richard." In the first of Poor Richard's almanacs, he wrote that his wife expected him to make some money with this almanac instead of wasting his time on other interests.

Poor Richard's Almanack quoted famous writers, proverbs, and mottos. Franklin, as Poor Richard, also included plenty of his

The first *Poor Richard's Almanack* sold well.

Poor Richard

Below are just a few of many sayings Benjamin Franklin wrote for *Poor Richard's Almanack.*

God helps them that help themselves.

One To-day is worth two To-Morrows.

Being ignorant is not so much a Shame, as being unwilling to learn.

The worst wheel of the cart makes the most noise.

Three may keep a secret, if two of them are dead.

Hunger never saw bad bread.

Haste makes Waste.

Well done is better than well said.

Diligence is the Mother of Good-Luck.

No gains without pains.

When the Well's dry, we know the worth of water.

Glass, China, and Reputation are easily crack'd, and never well mended.

A good example is the best sermon.

---

own advice. His sayings were straightforward and memorable. *Poor Richard* inspired readers to be honest, hardworking, and not wasteful.

Many families bought almanacs but not books. Books were costly. One reason was that, at this

Making His Fortune   39

time, the printing process was difficult and time consuming. In addition, most books had to be imported from Europe. But Franklin had always managed to buy books. He would almost rather go hungry than go without books. His business was successful. So he wanted to do something for the people of Philadelphia. He began to think about ways to encourage reading.

He and a group of friends had formed a club called the Junto. With them, he began to develop a collection of books for people to borrow. Members of the Junto and Franklin himself would also use such a collection. They already borrowed each other's books often. Then they talked about what they'd been reading.

> **It's a Fact!**
> The original collection of the books in Junto's library still exists.

Franklin and his friends set up their library in a small building. The building also served as a museum. It had displays of fossils, rocks, and other things. The Junto members called it the Library Company of Philadelphia. They donated some of the books themselves. They charged a small membership fee and used the money to order more

Because many colonial homes and shops were made of wood, fires were a terrible danger.

books from Europe. Members could borrow books whenever they wished. People who weren't members could rent books. This library was the first of its kind in North America. Franklin later remembered, "Reading became fashionable."

Meanwhile, Philadelphia was doing well. People were busily trading goods with other colonial cities and with Great Britain. Many new homes were being built. These homes and other buildings were heated by fireplaces. They were lit by candles and oil lamps. Fire was always a danger. So Franklin organized a firefighting company, the first fire department in North America. He thought people would fight fires better together than separately.

Chapter 3
Franklin of Philadelphia

In 1736 Franklin's son Franky died of smallpox. He was four years old. Smallpox was a common and deadly disease in the 1700s. Doctors had just learned how to protect people against it by inoculating them. This meant injecting them with a weak version of the disease. But many people did not yet believe that inoculating was safe.

Rumors flew in Philadelphia that Franklin had had Franky inoculated. In response, Franklin wrote a newspaper article. In it, he explained that his little boy had caught the infection "in the common way." He began finding out more about inoculation. And he began educating people about how it could protect them and their children.

That same year, the Pennsylvania Assembly hired Franklin to be assembly clerk. As clerk, Franklin attended all sessions and recorded what happened. He wrote down the new bills that were introduced and the new laws that were passed. The job could be boring. Franklin spent hours doodling at this desk, barely listening to the words drifting by.

The job did give him new business contacts, however. The bankers and other business owners Franklin met bought advertising in the *Gazette*. Franklin was also hugely successful with *Poor Richard's Almanack*. He sold ten thousand copies every year. *Poor Richard* was second only to the Bible in readership.

About a year later, Franklin was appointed deputy postmaster for North America. This was a royal appointment—meaning it came with the king's

> **IT'S A FACT!**
> Franklin used his influence and energy to improve life in Philadelphia. He set up a program to pave, clean, and light the streets. He raised money to build the city's first hospital. He helped establish a school that eventually became the University of Pennsylvania.

Franklin of Philadelphia   43

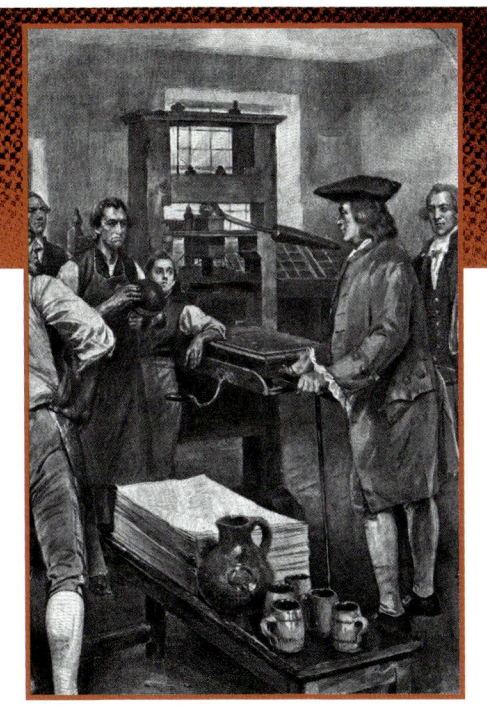

Franklin *(wearing hat)* used his skill as a printer to educate people on many subjects.

approval—and carried a large salary. Franklin improved postal service. For example, he increased the number of days mail was delivered. At the same time, he began to trim expenses.

Franklin's new jobs helped him better understand Pennsylvania's government. The real power was clearly four thousand miles away, in London. Years earlier, the king had made William Penn the proprietor of the colony. That meant he was the founder and chief landowner. Penn's three sons—Thomas, Richard, and John—stayed mainly in Britain. But they had inherited a lot of land in the colony. They also appointed the colony's governor and told him what to do. William Penn had given the Pennsylvania Assembly the right to make laws. But the proprietors could force the governor to veto (reject) those laws. The longer Franklin worked in Pennsylvania government, the more he disliked this proprietary system of power.

"Electrical Fluid"

Benjamin Franklin had many interests. He carefully watched the natural world. On one trip to the Appalachian Mountains, he saw that the layers of rock contained seashells. He concluded that the area must have been underwater sometime in the past. "It is certainly the wreck of a world we live on," he wrote to a friend.

In 1743 Franklin visited Dr. Archibald Spencer in Boston. Franklin watched Spencer carry out some electrical experiments. Franklin wrote, "They equally surpriz'd and pleas'd me."

The next year, Franklin invited Spencer to come to Philadelphia. Spencer did the experiments. Franklin bought some of Spencer's equipment. Then in 1746, the Library Company received a glass tube. It came with instructions on how to use it for electrical experiments. Franklin and the Library Company ordered copies of the glass tube.

Franklin of Philadelphia 45

THE FRANKLIN STOVE

The people of Philadelphia spent much of their time indoors, especially in cold weather. Mostly, they heated their homes with fires in fireplaces. But only the part of a room near the fire stayed warm. Most houses had many chilly spots and drafts.

Benjamin Franklin invented a stove that could warm houses better. The Franklin stove was made of iron. The stove took in fresh air from outside and heated it through a series of openings onto a small log fire. Then it circulated the heat throughout a room.

The Franklin stove not only kept an entire room warm but also saved on firewood.

At this time, electricity was a strange force that people were only just beginning to understand. Scientists were trying to explain it, but their ideas didn't satisfy Franklin. He and others saw that certain objects let electricity pass through, or conducted electricity, causing the force to move from one object to another. Other objects did not conduct electricity. Some scientists believed that different kinds of objects produced different kinds of "electrical fluid."

46   Benjamin Franklin

Several inventors had built devices to create electricity. One device was a large, glass jar, called a Leyden jar, that was filled with water or small pieces of lead. The jar was coated with a conducting material and connected by wires to a charged object. It could store a powerful electrical charge.

Franklin started his own electrical experiments. He set out the glass tubes and some glass jars. He sent electrical shocks through wood, paper, glass, and even his own fingers. He made his own hair stand on end. He lit candlewicks with electrical charges. He fired guns and rang bells electrically.

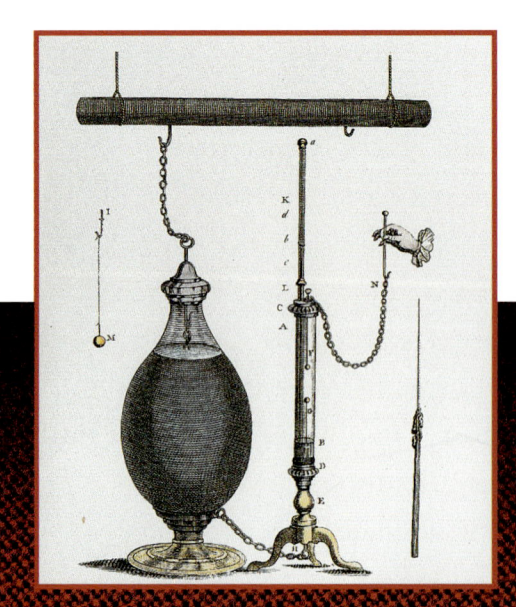

He drew a crooked, blue electrical flame from the top

Franklin performed many experiments and proposed many inventions in his lifetime. This illustration shows the Leyden jar he used for many electrical experiments.

of an egg. "My House was continually full for some time," he wrote, "with People who came to see these new Wonders."

The small electrical sparks reminded Franklin of lightning. Nobody really understood lightning. But many people had noticed that it seemed to act like electricity in many ways. Franklin wrote down twelve ways in which they were alike. He said that lightening and electricity gave off light and moved quickly. Their sparks tended to be crooked rather than straight. The electrical flames in the laboratory could burn holes through paper. And lightning could set buildings on fire. He noticed that pointed objects (such as knitting needles) drew the crooked blue flame. Lightning also seemed to be attracted to points.

Franklin guessed that lightning was a kind of big electrical spark. Some other scientists had guessed this too. But no one had found a way to prove it. Franklin continued to study electricity. He wanted to prove the connection between laboratory sparks and streaks of lightning.

A Close Call with the French

In 1743 Franklin and Deborah had a daughter, Sarah, whom they called Sally. William, who had become a handsome boy, was about thirteen years old. Franklin was doing well at home and in business.

The colonies were quickly growing in population. Immigrants from Great Britain and Europe arrived daily. Demand for printing work was increasing too. Franklin knew he could profit from this demand. He encouraged his apprentices and others to start printing shops in other cities. He offered one-third of the money needed to get started. In exchange, he would get one-third of the profits. He helped start printing businesses throughout eastern North America.

Franklin seemed full of energy and ideas. He wrote many letters. He exchanged letters with friends and people who were interested in the same things he was. In 1743 he wrote to a number of his contacts. He suggested that they all write letters and exchange them among themselves. That way they could more easily share their ideas about science, philosophy, and other matters. The group became known as the American

> **IT'S A FACT!**
> Franklin didn't patent, or formally claim, his inventions. He wanted people to use them freely to improve their lives.

Throughout his life, Franklin wrote many letters to friends and people he worked with.

Philosophical Society. A year later, Franklin organized a police force in Philadelphia. His corner of North America was becoming civilized.

At the same time, the French and British were fighting a war nearby. They battled for control of territory in Canada and the western frontier of the British colonies. With the help of many Indian nations, the French had the upper hand. In 1747 the French sailed up the Delaware River. They captured a ship about twenty miles below Philadelphia.

The war had come too close for comfort. Franklin knew Philadelphia had to be ready to defend itself. He suggested that the city form a militia. A militia is a group of citizens that is trained to fight during an emergency. He felt that being prepared for war would help keep peace. But many people in the city were Quakers. Their religion didn't allow wars or other violence. For this reason, many people were against Franklin. The main proprietor, the landowner Thomas Penn, was against him too. He didn't want Pennsylvanians to form a militia he didn't control.

In November of 1747, Franklin published a pamphlet entitled *Plain Truth*. In it, he criticized Thomas Penn and colonists who would do nothing to defend their own homes. Then Franklin called a meeting of the citizens of Philadelphia. At the meeting, about one thousand men volunteered to form a militia. The number grew to more than ten thousand men over the next few weeks. Using their own weapons, the militia volunteers began training. They spent their free time drilling and shooting at targets. They built walls and dug trenches to protect nearby farms and villages.

Franklin of Philadelphia 51

Franklin created this illustration for his pamphlet *Plain Truth*.

The French did not invade Philadelphia. In 1748 a peace treaty was signed and the crisis passed. Most people admired what Franklin had done. Even many Quakers came to see the value of the militia.
Thomas Penn thought that Franklin "had done much mischief." But Franklin was very popular. Penn knew he "must be treated with regard."

By this time, Franklin was forty-two. His printing shop was one of the most successful in

52   Benjamin Franklin

Pennsylvania. He had published the *Pennsylvania Gazette* and *Poor Richard's Almanack*. He had printed pamphlets and books, including the first novel ever printed in North America. It was called *Pamela*, by the British writer Samuel Richardson. He had money and a good reputation. It seemed like a good time to retire.

"Seizing the Lightning"

In 1748 Franklin gave responsibility for his printing shop to a friend, David Hall. Franklin continued to edit the *Gazette* and *Poor Richard's Almanack*. He was happy to have much more free time.

Electricity still fascinated him. In 1749 he came up with an experiment. It would prove that lightning and electricity were the same. The experimenter would have to put up a tall iron rod at the top of a building. Franklin had noticed that "the electrical fluid is attracted by points." So the rod must be sharply pointed. Then the experimenter would

It's a Fact!

To document his theory about electricity, Franklin once tried to kill a turkey using an electrical shock. By mistake, the shock hit Franklin and stunned him. The turkey lived. Franklin later wrote, "I meant to kill a turkey, and instead, I nearly killed a goose!"

Franklin of Philadelphia 53

climb up to the rod during a thunderstorm. He or she would hold a wire near the rod. Franklin believed that the wire would draw sparks from the rod. If it did, the storm was creating an electrical charge. A wax grip on the wire would prevent the experimenter from getting a shock.

In 1750 Franklin expanded his ideas into a small book, *Experiments and Observations on Electricity.* Many scientists wrote in Latin, but Franklin wrote in English. He used plain language that was easy to understand. His book was printed in Great Britain and also translated into German

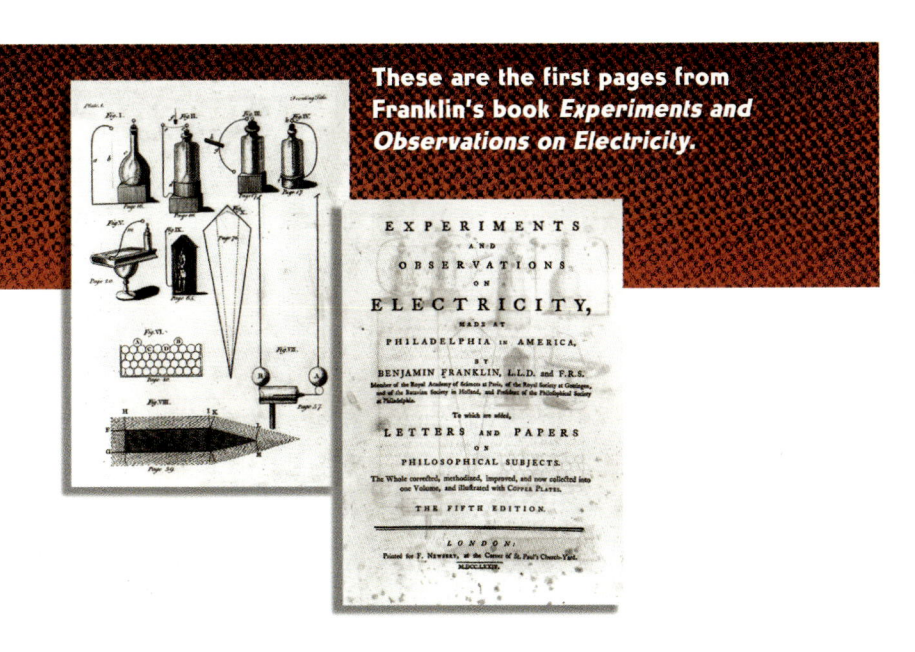

These are the first pages from Franklin's book *Experiments and Observations on Electricity.*

and Italian. A French scientist published the book in French. He hired an English-speaking scientist named Thomas d'Abilard to translate it.

D'Abilard became interested in the experiment. He decided to try it. He had a tall iron pole put on a wooden shed in the village of Marly la Ville. The town was just north of Paris, France. Then d'Abilard hired a French soldier named Coiffier to help him. On May 10, 1752, a heavy storm passed over Marly la Ville. Coiffier bravely crouched at the base of the pole. He kept moving a wire closer and closer to the pole and pulling it away again. Each time, blue sparks danced before his eyes. Onlookers were amazed. Coiffier, d'Abilard, and Franklin had proved that lightning and electricity were one and the same. Reports of their success made Franklin a celebrity all over Europe.

Franklin's lightning experiment resulted in a useful invention called the lightning rod. It would save buildings from fire caused by lightning. Lightning would go into the rod, down a wire, and safely into the ground.

Some people didn't think lightning rods would really protect people. Lightning rods drew electricity out of the air and into the ground. The Reverend

Franklin of Philadelphia 55

FRANKLIN'S KITE EXPERIMENT

Benjamin Franklin is famous for using a kite to prove that lightning is an electrical charge. He never put the story of that experiment in writing, however, but his friend, Joseph Priestley, did.

According to Priestley, Franklin believed that the iron rod in his experiment needed to be on a very high place. No rooftop in Philadelphia was high enough. So in June of 1752, Franklin decided to use a kite. With it, he could gain "access to the regions of thunder." (The experiment in France had taken place one month earlier, but Franklin had not yet heard about it.) Franklin's son William helped him raise the kite during a thunderstorm. Franklin then moved his knuckle close to a key tied to the kite string. When he did, he "perceived a very evident electric spark."

Thomas Prince of Boston worried this might lead to "more shocking Earthquakes." Besides, lightning might be part of God's plan. Was protecting your home from lightning going against God?

Despite the worries of some, many people in America and Europe put up lightning rods. Humans, livestock, and buildings were protected—all thanks to a gentleman from North America named Benjamin Franklin.

The Albany Congress

Because Franklin had cut back on his publishing work, he had time to get more involved in local politics. He easily won election to the Pennsylvania Assembly in 1751. The assembly only made laws for Pennsylvania. But all the colonies would need defense if war with the French broke out again. They would need a united government.

The last war against France had been expensive for Britain. The British government wanted the colonists to pay some of the costs. The British also wanted the colonists to make peace with Native Americans on the frontier. In June of 1754, delegates (representatives) from the colonies met to discuss these issues. Franklin and three other men were the delegates for Pennsylvania.

The meeting took place in Albany, New York. It came to be called the Albany Congress. At the congress, Franklin presented a "Plan of Union." He showed how the colonies could unite for self-defense. He published a cartoon by an unknown artist. It showed a snake divided into parts, with each part labeled as a colony. "Join, or Die," the cartoon warned.

Franklin's Plan of Union was intended to strengthen the colonies. Franklin believed it would also help Great Britain if its American colonies were stronger. None of the colonial assemblies voted for the Plan of Union. They feared that any one colony might lose power in a united government. The British government rejected the plan too. The British feared that Britain might lose control over its colonies if they united.

When this cartoon appeared in *The Pennsylvania Gazette* on May 9, 1754, it became the first political cartoon to come from the colonies.

A battle of the French and Indian War. The man on horseback is an inexperienced young officer named George Washington.

The French and British began fighting again in 1756. Native Americans were still on the side of France. Native Americans burned down villages, destroyed homes, and murdered settlers on the Pennsylvania frontier.

The war came to be known as the French and Indian War. How could Pennsylvania defend itself during this war? The militia Franklin had formed was a good start. But it needed money for guns and other supplies. The Pennsylvania Assembly decided to place a new tax on land. This included the lands of the proprietors. But the proprietors ordered the governor to veto the new tax law.

Many colonists were disgusted. In 1757 the assembly asked Franklin to go to Great Britain. One of his tasks would be to meet with the Penns. He would try to convince them to agree to pay taxes on their land.

Chapter 4
A Mission in Britain

Franklin sailed for London in June. His twenty-seven-year-old son, William, went with him. Deborah and Sally didn't join them. Deborah was afraid of sailing across the ocean.

In London, Franklin and William rented rooms from Margaret Stevenson, a widow. Mrs. Stevenson had a fine house near the Thames River that runs through London. Setting up meetings with the Penns and other British officials would take time. So the Franklins settled in for a long stay. With Franklin were two servants he had brought from Philadelphia.

It's a Fact!
The London house in which Franklin stayed was at 36 Craven Street. It is being turned into an interactive exhibit and living history site.

60   Benjamin Franklin

This portrait shows how Benjamin Franklin looked a few years before he traveled to London.

The weeks slipped by. Franklin again found London to his liking. He made many close friends. He sent home presents, including china, tableware, and tablecloths for Deborah and a musical instrument called a harpsichord for Sally.

TAXING THE PROPRIETORS

For many months, the Penns refused to meet with Franklin. Finally, they agreed to see him. But they would not agree to pay taxes on their land in Pennsylvania. They argued that their power in Pennsylvania came directly from the king. They could veto any tax they wished.

Franklin later wrote that Thomas Penn was rude and insulting. Franklin wrote of his lack of respect for Penn. He said that he felt a more "thorough contempt for him, than I ever before felt for any man living." Unfortunately, Thomas Penn got his hands on a copy of this letter. He was furious and made Franklin his sworn enemy.

Franklin had failed with the Penns. So he began meeting with members of Parliament—Britain's governing body. Franklin met with dozens of officials. He tried to convince them that the colony had a right to tax the proprietors. Under pen names, he wrote articles for British newspapers. Franklin was a very good writer, and he was able to convince many important people to side with the colonists.

In April of 1759, the Pennsylvania Assembly passed a bill. It would raise a lot of money for the colony's defense. This bill again included taxes on the lands of the proprietors. Pennsylvania's governor approved the bill against the wishes of Thomas Penn.

The Penns turned to the Privy Council. This was a powerful group of British advisers. The Penns asked the council to reject the bill. Franklin went to the Privy Council too. He argued that the proprietors' lands would be taxed at the same rate as any other land. The Privy Council decided in favor of Pennsylvania. The proprietors began paying taxes on

Franklin the Musician

Benjamin Franklin loved music. He played several musical instruments, including the violin and the harp. In 1761 he invented a new musical instrument, the glass armonica. It was based on an older instrument called the Glasspiel. The armonica was a set of spinning cups. Its sound was like that made when a finger is rubbed around the rim of a water-filled glass. The best composers of the time—including Mozart and Beethoven—wrote short pieces for the armonica. Audiences flocked to hear concerts of armonica music. Unfortunately, the armonica was fragile. Playing it was hard on musicians' hands. By the 1800s, the armonica was no longer used.

their American lands for the first time ever. Against heavy odds, Franklin had won a huge argument with the British government in favor of the Americans.

Call for a Royal Takeover

Franklin sailed for Pennsylvania in August 1763. His son, William, left London soon after for New Jersey.

Educated in Britain, William had impressed the British, who named him governor of that colony.

People in Pennsylvania admired Franklin. He seemed to know how to get things done abroad. He had even become Doctor Franklin, when two British universities gave him honorary degrees. Franklin had been elected to the Pennsylvania Assembly every year he spent in London. He became the assembly's leader when he returned.

John Penn had become governor of Pennsylvania. He wrote to his brother Thomas, blaming Franklin for local unrest. "While [Franklin] was in England there was at least an appearance of Peace and Quietness," he said in his letter. "But since his return, the old Sparks are again blown up."

Franklin criticized Governor Penn's actions and told a friend that Penn had lost the assembly's approval. Franklin and others wanted to remove the Penns from power. They wanted Pennsylvania to be ruled directly by the king and Parliament. Then perhaps the people would have more liberty.

But not everyone wanted a change to the government. Some people attacked Franklin personally. They claimed he wanted a royal government because he profited by it. After all, his royal appointment as postmaster included a large salary. These people said that Franklin was just greedy and power hungry. He did not really care about what was best for Pennsylvania. Franklin published a rejection of these charges. Still, in the election of 1764, he lost his seat in the assembly, where he had served for thirteen years.

But many candidates who wanted a change in government were elected. The assembly members voted for such a change. They wrote a petition, a letter that they all signed. They asked the king "to resume the Government of this Province." Then they chose Franklin to return to Great Britain with the petition. He would represent Pennsylvania in its effort to end the proprietors' power.

THE STAMP ACT

On November 7, 1764, Franklin left again for London. Still refusing to sail overseas, Deborah stayed behind. Franklin again took up lodgings with Mrs. Stevenson. He made his familiar rounds of old friends. He visited one high official after another. He asked that the Pennsylvania petition for a change of government be heard. He also became an agent for other colonies. He represented Georgia, New Jersey, and Massachusetts.

Many people in Great Britain opened their doors to Franklin. He was well known to important people. Scientists, teachers, bankers, ministers, lords, and ladies knew him. He walked through London and toured the hilly countryside.

Few British officials had time for Franklin's petition. They had other problems. Great Britain had won the war with the French in North America in 1763. The British got control of Canada and added these holdings to their other colonies. But the war had been the costliest in British history so far. It had drained the British treasury. Also, Britain had to defend a much bigger territory in North America. The government needed to double the number of British troops on the continent.

Parliament needed money, and it expected the colonies to share in the cost of defense. So, in March of 1765, Parliament passed a new tax called the Stamp Act. The Stamp Act required a stamp to be placed on legal documents and other paper products, including newspapers and playing cards. Colonists would have to pay for the stamps. Any documents that did not carry the stamp would be illegal.

66   Benjamin Franklin

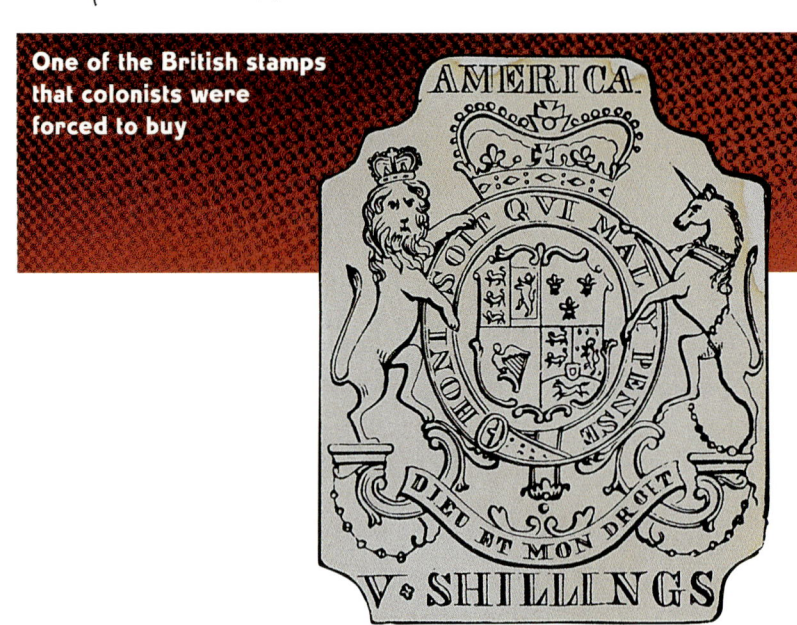

One of the British stamps that colonists were forced to buy

Colonists were furious. They hadn't had a vote in the Stamp Act. They had no representatives in Parliament. They felt the act was "taxation without representation." In many cities, colonists refused to buy the stamps. Some people threatened those who had to sell the stamps. Many people fought against the Stamp Act. As a result, it could not be enforced.

These events surprised Franklin, who was still in London. At first, a small tax on documents didn't seem so bad to him. Instead of opposing the Stamp Act, he suggested that colonists live more simply. Then they could afford to pay the tax.

Some colonists saw this as a betrayal. Some even believed Franklin had helped to create the Stamp Act. He gained many enemies in Pennsylvania. Some friends feared for Deborah Franklin's safety. They tried to convince her to leave Philadelphia. Instead, she stayed home. She locked the door and kept a pistol ready. In September, a mob tried to attack the Franklin house, but friends of the Franklins stopped them.

The following month, the colonists held a Stamp Act congress. It said that the tax was not the main issue. More important was whether or not Parliament could tax the colonies without their consent.

The congress demanded the repeal, or end, of the Stamp Act. In addition, colonists began to boycott (refuse to buy) British goods. The boycott worried British merchants and manufacturers. It was clear that the boycott was hurting them. Soon they, too, began asking for repeal of the Stamp Act.

In London, Franklin wrote newspaper articles defending the colonies. He joined the call for repeal. In February of 1766, he testified before Parliament. He warned that the colonies might begin an armed rebellion if the Stamp Act was not repealed.

Colonists in Boston protest the Stamp Act by burning stamped documents in a bonfire.

Parliament did repeal the Stamp Act. But on the same day, it passed a law called the Declaratory Act. It said that Parliament had the power "to bind the Colonies and people of America in all cases whatsoever." The colonies had shaken off the Stamp Act. Yet Parliament quickly reminded them that Parliament could pass another law like it at any time. Also, Parliament refused to even consider the takeover of Pennsylvania by the royal government.

CHAPTER 5

More Trouble in the Colonies

In June of 1767, the British chancellor, or head of the treasury, passed new duties (import taxes) on the colonists. The chancellor's name was Charles Townshend. The duties were called the Townshend duties. Colonists would have to pay duties to import glass, lead, paper, paint, and tea. These new duties angered some colonists, who quickly organized another boycott.

The assembly of Massachusetts called for united action by all the colonies. Governor Thomas Hutchinson responded by dissolving the assembly. He said it could not meet again.

People were angry about the Townshend duties and Hutchinson's response. In Boston, people began rioting. One Bostonian, Samuel Adams, formed the Sons of Liberty. This was a secret organization that

British redcoats march into Boston to enforce new tax laws.

attacked British officials and tax collectors. Adams gave thundering speeches. He inspired many colonists to demand their independence from the king. Acts of rebellion, rioting, and arson (setting fires on purpose) spread throughout the colonies.

News of the revolt soon reached Great Britain. This time, the British did not repeal the taxes. Instead, they sent troops. The soldiers were known as redcoats because of their bright red uniforms. They patrolled the streets and guarded roads and

More Trouble in the Colonies 71

bridges. They began building forts outside major cities. They stayed in Boston for several years. The colonists grew angrier and angrier. The Sons of Liberty stepped up their attacks. They even burned Governor Hutchinson's house.

On March 5, 1770, some Bostonians began taunting British soldiers. The soldiers were on guard outside the Boston Customs House. A crowd gathered and began throwing snowballs and chunks of ice at the soldiers. The troops became nervous. They fired into the crowd and killed five people. This tragedy later came to be known as the Boston Massacre.

Franklin was still in London. He felt he should smooth relations between the British government and the colonies. He must persuade the British to understand the colonists' point of view. He must also do something about Governor Hutchinson, who seemed to be losing control of Massachusetts.

GOVERNOR HUTCHINSON'S LETTERS

Sometime in late 1772, Franklin was secretly given some private letters. The letters were written by several important men of Massachusetts. Two of them were Governor Thomas Hutchinson and his deputy governor, Andrew Oliver. Franklin opened and read the letters, which had been written to a member of Parliament named Thomas Whately in 1768 and 1769. Whately had since died. In the letters, Hutchinson wrote that American colonists should not have the same rights as British citizens. He didn't think a colony should "enjoy all the liberty of the parent state."

Franklin knew Hutchinson's words would anger the people of Massachusetts. He also knew that the colony needed to replace Hutchinson before peace could be restored.

In December of 1772, Franklin sent the letters to Thomas Cushing. Cushing was a member of the Massachusetts Assembly. Franklin asked Cushing not to publish the letters in a newspaper. Instead, Cushing should show them to just a few members of the assembly. Franklin wanted those men to use the letters carefully against Hutchinson. Cushing tried to follow Franklin's instructions, but he soon lost control of the letters. They passed through many hands. Some members of the assembly wanted the letters made public.

In June of 1773, the Hutchinson letters were read aloud in the assembly. They were recorded by the assembly clerk. Soon afterward, the letters were reported in the press. People's feelings against Hutchinson grew. The Massachusetts Assembly quickly voted to petition the king. The petition said Hutchinson and Oliver were "chargeable with causing misery and bloodshed." It asked the king to "remove them from their posts." It would, of course, be Franklin's job to present the petitions in London.

Scolding Doctor Franklin

Meanwhile, the boycott of the Townshend duties continued. The public outcry eventually ended most of the import duties, except for the duty on tea. But the relationship between Great Britain and its colonies remained tense. The British heard that Hutchinson's letters had been published in America. This made matters worse. Gossip swirled about London. Someone had stolen the letters, but who? Some people suspected Whately's brother William and William's friend John Temple. Temple was furious over the rumors. He blamed William Whately and challenged him to a secret fight between gentlemen, called a duel, using swords as the weapons. The two men met in Hyde Park in

London. Temple wounded Whately twice before they agreed to lay down their swords.

In December of 1773, a group of colonists gathered at Boston Harbor in Massachusetts. They would not accept the duty on tea. To make their point, the group slipped aboard three British merchant ships. They dumped 342 crates of tea into the water. News of the "Boston Tea Party" quickly reached London. The British were outraged. Franklin was "grieved to hear of mobs and violence."

> **IT'S A FACT!**
> Franklin offered to pay for the ruined tea out of his own pocket. He thought this action would ease the tension between the colonies and Great Britain.

Franklin also heard about the duel between Whately and Temple. So he decided to admit his responsibility. He announced in a London newspaper that he had sent the Hutchinson letters to Massachusetts. Many people in Britain saw Franklin's act as treason—the crime of betraying one's country by helping an enemy. They did not disapprove of Hutchinson and Oliver for their letters. Instead, they disapproved of Franklin for making the letters public.

Rebels empty crates of tea into Boston Harbor. This protest against the British-imposed tax on tea came to be known as the Boston Tea Party.

A hearing was held on January 29, 1774. Alexander Wedderburn spoke for the British government. He accused Franklin of trickery and dishonesty, and he attacked the people of Massachusetts as well. He said Franklin acted as if America were "a foreign independent state." Franklin refused to argue against the charges. He seemed a symbol of American rebellion.

Thomas Hutchinson and Andrew Oliver were quickly cleared. But Franklin was publicly humiliated. He was removed as deputy postmaster of North America, and William Whately sued him. Some thought Parliament would try to prove that

Franklin had committed treason. In any case, Franklin's reputation in Britain was shattered.

Franklin no longer believed that the colonies and Great Britain could get along. Yet he dreaded war. He spent the next months asking for complete independence for the colonies. "Recall your forces," he advised Britain's leaders. "Renounce your pretensions to Tax us, [and] refund the duties you have extorted." By this time, very few British leaders would listen to Franklin.

Not long after, Franklin got word that his wife, Deborah, had died. The cause may have been a stroke. He had not seen her for more than ten years. Clearly, he could do nothing more in London. On March 21, 1775, Benjamin Franklin sailed for home.

Chapter 6
Shots Heard 'Round the World

Franklin's life was filled with trouble. Still, he closely watched everything around him aboard ship. He had often made notes on improving sails and ship designs. On this trip, as he crossed the Atlantic Ocean from Britain to North America, he investigated a current of water. Some seamen believed this current swept eastward across the Atlantic Ocean. The ever-curious Franklin took the temperature of the air and water each day. In doing so, he found that the current was warm. He had found evidence of what he named the Gulf Stream, which brings warm air to northwestern Europe, including Britain.

While Franklin was on his way back to North America, British troops still occupied Boston. Feelings against them ran high. Many colonists

Colonial minutemen from Stockbridge, Massachusetts, prepare for war.

believed they needed to be ready to defend themselves against the British at a minute's notice. Some formed minuteman units. These small militias began training and gathering weapons.

On April 19, 1775, British troops marched out of Boston toward the nearby town of Concord. Their mission was to seize a stockpile of weapons reported to be there. The redcoats marched through the town of Lexington on their way to Concord. There, some colonists took up positions behind rocks and trees and fired at them. The British marched in the open in bright red uniforms. They made easy targets. More than 250 of them were killed or wounded.

The British responded by burning farms and looting homes. They sent more troops to Boston, while the British army in Canada got ready to march down the Hudson River Valley to attack New York. Throughout New England, colonists quickly formed militias to fight the British. But with no regular army, the colonists were outgunned.

Franklin arrived in Philadelphia in May of 1775. He found the colonies surprisingly united against the British. "I found at my arrival all

Uniformed British soldiers fight the colonial minutemen in the Battle of Lexington on April 19, 1775. This conflict was the first of the American Revolution.

America... busily employed in learning the use of Arms," he wrote. Years earlier, his Plan of Union had met opposition. This time, the colonies were rallying around a common cause. "The Unanimity is amazing," he wrote.

Franklin was almost seventy and had grown weak. But he believed in the colonies' right to govern themselves. He would do what he could to help reach that goal. He was asked to serve on the Pennsylvania Committee of Safety. The committee would help prepare the defenses of Pennsylvania. Franklin accepted. He also agreed to be a delegate to the Second Continental Congress. The congress would conduct the war and establish a foreign policy for the colonists. It met in Philadelphia just five days after his return from London.

The Continental Congress made some last attempts to make up with Great Britain. But the British would not cooperate. In August, King George III formally declared the colonies to be in rebellion.

"REBELLION TO TYRANTS"

Small groups of colonists had been clashing with British troops but with little gain. Congress clearly needed to organize them into one army. It appointed George Washington of Virginia to be commander in chief. Franklin was assigned to help buy supplies for Washington's men.

Washington set up headquarters in Cambridge, Massachusetts, where he met with Franklin in October of 1775. Washington was trying to organize an army of twenty thousand men. To defeat the British, the army must be well disciplined and well equipped. Washington asked for guns, gunpowder, flints, shoes, blankets, tents, clothing, food, horses, and wagons, among other things.

Franklin returned to Philadelphia with Washington's requests. The job ahead of him must have seemed almost impossible. How could the colonists produce all these supplies for so many soldiers? They owned farms, not factories. For decades they had bought their manufactured goods from Britain. Congress had no money to buy supplies from abroad. Besides, the British navy was patrolling the coast. This kept merchant ships out of colonial harbors.

Clearly, congress needed allies–other countries to help them. Perhaps, the French would help. They had long been enemies with Britain. Franklin met secretly with a member of the French court

A fleet of British ships surrounds Boston Harbor.

who was visiting the colonies. But the French didn't want to anger the British by helping the colonists.

Within Franklin's family, turmoil lurked. His son, William, still held his royal appointment as governor of New Jersey and maintained his loyalty to Britain. In January of 1776, Congress stripped him of his title and put him under house arrest. (This meant he could live in his house but not leave it.) Franklin had put his own life in danger to fight for independence. He was deeply angry that William would not join the cause. He did nothing to help his son get free.

Shots Heard 'Round the World 83

Congress continued the search for allies. The settlers in British-controlled Canada were one possibility. Many were French, and they might be willing to challenge the British. In March, Congress asked Franklin to travel to Canada. He would try to make an alliance with the French Canadians.

Franklin set out with two other men from New York on April 2, 1776. The group traveled along the Hudson River and Lake Champlain to the Canadian border. The journey was long and hard. Franklin often felt ill. Heavy snow covered the ground, and everyone shivered in the freezing air.

> **IT'S A FACT!**
> To protect himself from the cold, Franklin began to wear a small, raccoon skin fur cap. He first wore it during his journey to Canada.

Franklin's group found that British troops had abandoned Montreal, the main French Canadian city. They had moved to a stronger position in Quebec City. Colonist soldiers in Montreal were led by General Benedict Arnold. The army was cold and hungry, and many of the men were suffering from smallpox. Under these conditions, Arnold could not pursue the British.

Franklin lent Arnold some of his own money to buy supplies. Then he and his companions met with French Canadians in the area. They tried to get loans for the Continental Army (the colonists' army). Franklin hoped some of the Canadians would help the colonists fight the British. They might even fight to win their own independence from Great Britain.

But up to this point, the French Canadians had been well treated by the British. They refused to give help. Then Franklin's group learned that the British had brought even more troops to Quebec City. The colonists realized that Montreal might come under attack soon. They did not want to be caught behind enemy lines and taken prisoner. They quickly left, knowing their mission had been a cold and miserable failure.

Declaring Independence

Franklin returned to Philadelphia. He found that many people there were giving up the fight. The British seemed too strong. The Continental Army was too small and too disorganized. The militia units were having no effect on British positions. The British navy was sailing up and down the coast, bombarding ports, and stopping supplies from getting through.

The members of the Continental Congress knew that failure would mean their own ruin. Franklin knew it too. Somehow, Congress had to turn this small rebellion into a full-scale revolution. Their best hope was to gain allies.

The French might be willing to join their cause if Congress formally declared independence. So Congress formed another committee and appointed five members. They were Thomas Jefferson, Roger Sherman, Robert Livingston, John Adams, and

Working together on the Declaration of Independence are, *left to right:* **Thomas Jefferson, Roger Sherman, Benjamin Franklin, Robert Livingston, and John Adams.**

Benjamin Franklin. The committee's job was to prepare a declaration of independence.

Jefferson wrote the first draft of the Declaration of Independence during two weeks of June 1776. It said that the British king had taken away the colonists' natural rights to life, liberty, and the pursuit of happiness. It also said that its signers were forming a new country: the United States of America.

Franklin and the other members of the committee suggested some changes to Jefferson's draft. Then the committee sent it to the Second Continental Congress. On July 2, 1776, the congress voted to adopt the document with some changes. Two days later, on July 4, the congress accepted the final version. On August 2, Benjamin Franklin and fifty-five other members of the congress signed their names to the Declaration of Independence. In doing it, they put their own lives on the line for the sake of creating a new nation.

CHAPTER 7
Working for a New Nation

On August 27, 1776, General Washington and the Continental Army lost an important battle. A much larger British force had defeated them at Long Island, New York. The British took control of this busy and important harbor.

Despite this victory, many British realized the war would be long and hard. They had more soldiers than the colonists, but the colonists were scattered along a huge area. And the colonists were fighting in their own land, which they knew well. They did not fight in the open like the British. Instead, they made small-scale attacks that confused the British commanders.

Victory for the British would also bring problems for them. If they won the war, the rebellion would probably continue to simmer. They

88 Benjamin Franklin

would have to occupy North America for a long time. Keeping control would be costly, and the colonies would continue to gain strength. Its overall population was growing with new immigrants from Britain and other parts of Europe.

So the British asked to meet with members of the Continental Congress. Congress sent Benjamin Franklin, John Adams, and Edward Rutledge as its representatives.

At the meeting, Franklin told the British that the colonists demanded independence. Without it, they would agree to nothing. With it, the war could

This portrait of Benjamin Franklin was painted by British artist David Martin.

end. The United States might even become allies of Britain. The two nations would create a powerful partnership. The British Empire could remain the strongest and richest in the world.

The British representatives suggested a different deal. The leaders of the rebellion could be pardoned for their actions. Britain might end the taxes and other laws that the colonists opposed, but the colonies would remain colonies.

Franklin and his two companions listened, then politely left. The war would probably continue for a long time. They had one simple demand—complete independence. But independence was the one thing the British would not grant.

Sailing Eastward Again

A few months before the meeting with the British, the Continental Congress had sent Silas Deane as its representative to France. Deane's mission was to convince the French government to lend money to the colonists. He also met with French merchants. He was to arrange the secret shipment of arms and supplies across the Atlantic.

Deane's mission was not going well, however. The French didn't want another war with Great

Britain. They didn't think the colonists' rebellion was going to succeed. They weren't even sure they wanted it to succeed. How would French citizens react to the Americans defeating King George III? They might be inspired to rise up against their king, Louis XVI.

Deane was struggling, so Congress decided to send help. Again the delegates called on Benjamin Franklin. He would be well received in Europe, where he was famous as the man who had discovered the secrets of electricity and who had invented the lightning rod.

Franklin agreed to the assignment and set out in October of 1776. Two of his grandsons joined him: William Temple Franklin (William's son) and Benjamin Franklin Bache (Sally's son). Their journey across the sea was risky. The British navy controlled the Atlantic. But no British ship stopped them. They landed on the western coast of France in late November and then traveled by coach to Paris.

News of Franklin's arrival quickly spread throughout France and even to Britain. The British realized that Franklin would try to persuade France to give aid to the colonists. They

Franklin and his two grandsons are greeted by a crowd of French admirers.

protested to the French government, demanding that it force Franklin to leave. The French refused.

When Franklin reached Paris, he wrote to the Count de Vergennes. Vergennes was the foreign minister of King Louis XVI. Franklin came right to the point. He wanted to negotiate a treaty of friendship between the French king and the colonists.

Vergennes refused to consider a treaty. That would mean France was an official ally of the colonists. The British would become even angrier.

But Vergennes didn't want to turn Franklin away empty-handed. So he agreed to open French ports to American ships. This would allow Americans to trade freely with French merchants. He also agreed to aid American privateers (sailing ships commissioned by the Continental Congress to raid British merchant ships). They could sell their captured goods in French ports.

Franklin accepted these offers. He thought the French still might be talked into signing a treaty. But it would take time. So Franklin settled down in the town of Passy in the hills just west of Paris. He rented a fine old house that belonged to Donatien de Chaumont. De Chaumont was a wealthy businessman who was already selling arms to the colonists.

LIVING IN PASSY

Franklin knew that he would have to be careful and polite. He had a sensitive role to play. He worked to win acceptance among the French. He invited important people to eat at his home. He accepted invitations to their homes. Each day and evening, he met with merchants, government officials, writers, and scientists. He tried to convince these important people to support the American Revolution.

Working for a New Nation   93

Over time, Franklin became a celebrity in France. People everywhere knew who he was. They recognized his face from the many paintings of Franklin by popular French artists. Hundreds of prints and engravings were produced in mass quantities. Thousands of French people had

BEN'S BIFOCALS

"I wear my Spectacles constantly," Benjamin Franklin once told a friend. This often caused a problem, however. For example, he had trouble seeing at large dinner parties. He needed his glasses to see the food in front of him. But with his glasses on, he couldn't see the faces of people at the table very well.

To avoid taking his eyeglasses off constantly, Franklin ordered some special lenses. Only the lower half was made to correct his vision. The upper half was clear glass. Wearing these lenses, "I have only to move my Eyes up or down, as I want to see distinctly far or near," he explained. Result: Franklin had invented bifocals.

Franklin was living in France at the time. His bifocals helped him understand French, which he spoke poorly. "When one's Ears are not well accustomed to the Sounds of a Language," he wrote, "a Sight of the Movements in the Features of him that speaks helps to explain."

> **IT'S A FACT!**
>
> In Paris, Franklin went to great effort to beef up his image by writing funny letters and entertaining people with his clever stories. For wealthy Parisians, who were stuck with the stuffiness of the royal court, the old man was new and radical.

portraits of Benjamin Franklin in their homes.

The French loved Franklin because he was an enemy of Britain, France's longtime rival. And Franklin represented liberties that the common people of France didn't enjoy under their own king. Franklin wore simple clothes, not fancy court dress. He seemed a friendly old gentleman, like a kind uncle or grandfather. Many people called him "Papa Franklin."

As 1777 wore on, the war in North America was going badly. The British marched on Philadelphia and captured it. They took over Franklin's house and turned it into a barracks—a place for soldiers to live. The British also had spies in France who were following Franklin's every move. These spies reported on Franklin's meetings with French officials. They even read his letters. One spy, Dr. Edward Bancroft, was an old friend of Franklin's. He lived with Franklin in the house in Passy.

VICTORY AND TREATY

In the fall of 1777, the British planned an attack on the Hudson River Valley of New York. One British army would march from the north. Another would march from the south. The two armies were supposed to capture forts along the river. Then they would meet one another. These actions would split the colonies in two.

The southern army never received its orders, however. The Continental Army met the northern force at Saratoga, New York. The British surrendered on October 17, 1777. The Continental Army had won a huge victory against the redcoats. Before this battle, the redcoats had seemed unbeatable.

The victory at Saratoga changed everything. Franklin sent the news to every important French official he knew, including the Count de Vergennes. The French realized that this American Revolution might succeed. King Louis sent word to Franklin that he would listen to any proposals Franklin might offer.

Franklin suggested an alliance of the Americans with France against Great Britain. The

Franklin became a favorite visitor to the French court.

French accepted. On February 6, 1778, Franklin signed agreements with the government of France. The Treaty of Amity and Commerce allowed the French to give all necessary aid to the Americans. This aid included money, arms, and other supplies. The Treaty of Alliance would ally the United States with France if a war broke out between France and Great Britain. The Continental Congress ratified, or approved, these agreements in May of 1778. French arms, soldiers, and military leaders began to journey across the Atlantic to help the colonists.

The support of France turned the tide of the American Revolution. The British continued to fight. They captured cities and burned homes. But

Working for a New Nation

the French sent their best generals and admirals to help the Americans. And the colonists showed that they were better fighters than anyone had expected.

In the summer of 1781, a French fleet sailed to the mouth of Chesapeake Bay along the coast of Virginia. The fleet trapped a British army at Yorktown, Virginia, on the James River. Washington hurried to Yorktown with his army. The colonists bombed the British from land and sea. Finally, on October 19, the British surrendered.

Franklin, who had remained in Passy, rejoiced

Lord Charles Cornwallis surrenders by handing his sword to George Washington in Yorktown, Virginia.

when he received this news. The victory at Yorktown proved decisive. After six years of fighting, independence finally had been won!

Franklin, along with John Adams and John Jay, began negotiating another treaty. This treaty was with the British. The Americans demanded independence for the United States. The British and the Americans signed two treaties on November 30, 1782, and on September 3, 1783. These treaties formally ended the war.

Chapter 8
A Last Journey Home

By this time, Franklin was tired, and he wanted to go home to the new United States of America. But the Continental Congress asked him to remain in France a while longer. He realized his last years were approaching. In 1784 he wrote to a friend in Great Britain, "I look upon Death to be as necessary to our Constitution as Sleep. We shall rise refreshed in the Morning."

In May of 1785, the Continental Congress sent a message to the seventy-nine-year-old Franklin. It said his duties as diplomat to France were finally finished. Franklin prepared to return home. He packed more than one hundred boxes full of his possessions. On July 12, nearly everyone in Passy turned out to say good-bye.

100 Benjamin Franklin

Franklin sometimes experienced pain in his legs. He found it difficult to walk or even to ride in a coach. So he rode in a litter (a chair carried by two men) to the coast. Then he took a ship across the English Channel to Southampton, a port in southern Britain. This time, he stayed in Great Britain only a few days. Many of his British friends came to Southampton to greet him. He met briefly with his son, William. William had been released from his wartime imprisonment and had chosen to

Franklin received a welcome home greeting in Philadelphia, when he arrived in 1785.

live in Britain. Franklin could not fully forgive him for siding against America in the war. The two greeted one another cautiously. On July 28, Franklin sailed for home.

Creating the Constitution

Back home in Philadelphia, Franklin met old friends. He carried on experiments and played with his grandchildren. At night he enjoyed reading or writing. He liked playing chess or cards with the many guests who came to call.

Franklin's health had begun to fail. His body grew weaker. Still, he kept on inventing. He built a device to pluck books from high library shelves. He built a small fan into a chair to keep himself cool as he read. He built a clock and a device that automatically copied out letters as they were written. He installed a device that allowed him to lock his bedroom door without getting out of his bed.

Meanwhile, the new United States of America was making do with a government that dated to wartime. But a better system was clearly needed. In May of 1787, a Constitutional Convention began in Philadelphia. Its purpose was to build a new system of government.

Delegates talk at the Constitutional Convention in Philadelphia in 1787. Benjamin Franklin is seated *(bottom left).*

Pennsylvania sent Franklin as a delegate. The convention's delegates fought over the details of a constitution. Franklin watched from his chair. He made suggestions and calmed the arguments. One of his suggestions was that the nation's leaders serve as unpaid volunteers. A lust for power and money had corrupted the British government. Franklin didn't want the same thing to happen to leaders of the United States. The delegates did not accept his suggestion, however.

Franklin also called for a compromise (an

agreement in which both sides give up some of their demands) in the way power would be split up. Some delegates thought all the states should be equal in power. Some thought power should be based on the number of people living in a state, so that the small states would have less power than the big states. Franklin's compromise led to the modern-day system of a congress with two houses. In the U.S. Senate, every state has two senators. In the U.S. House of Representatives, states with more people have more representatives. Both the Senate and the House make up the U.S. Congress.

A Rising Sun

Many compromises had to be made while the constitution was being talked about. Over time, the final constitution took shape. The delegates still disagreed on some points. But the constitution needed the public support of every delegate. Then it would be accepted by the new nation. Franklin still had some concerns about the constitution. But he approved of it as a whole. "The opinions I have ... of its errors I sacrifice to the public good ... ," Franklin told the delegates. He said he hoped every delegate would approve it. His wise

104 Benjamin Franklin

> **IT'S A FACT!**
> **Franklin is the only person to have signed four major documents of early American history. These documents are the Declaration of Independence (1776), the U.S. Constitution (1787), the Treaty of Alliance with France (1778), and the Treaty of Paris with Britain (1783).**

advice gave a needed boost to the passing of the new U.S. Constitution.

Throughout the convention, Franklin was weak and often in pain. He had had a long and useful life. He could face death with few regrets. As he wrote to a friend, "Having seen during a long life a good deal of this world, I feel a growing curiosity to be acquainted with some other."

In his final years, he put his energy toward a new cause—the ending of slavery. He became president of the first U.S. antislavery group and sent Congress a petition, or request, to end slavery quickly. Slave owners in Congress objected to the petition. One even went so far as to try to prove that the Bible approved of slavery. In response, just weeks before his death, Franklin wrote a clever and entertaining answer that made fun of the slave owner's point of view.

A Last Journey Home

On April 17, 1790, Benjamin Franklin died in his bed at home. More than twenty thousand people from Philadelphia and other cities went to his funeral. Franklin was honored with speeches, long articles in newspapers, and pieces of art made of him by sculptors and painters.

Benjamin Franklin had arrived in Philadelphia as a young and hungry runaway. By his life's end, he had become one of his nation's Founding Fathers. He was a world-renowned scientist. He was a beloved mentor to a new generation of Americans. At the Constitutional Convention, he had called the United States a "rising sun." He left behind police watches, fire-fighting companies, libraries, an improved postal system, and countless other contributions and inventions. Through his many efforts, the new United States got a good start to become a great nation.

Glossary

British rule: Britain ruled many colonies around the world. It had colonies in Asia, Africa, North America, and South America and claimed the entire continent of Australia. Most of these colonies got free of British rule in the 1900s.

colony: a territory set up by a larger country that is far away. Britain set up thirteen colonies along the eastern coast of North America. These colonies would become the first states of the United States.

congress: a formal meeting of people to set policies or make laws. During and after the American Revolution, several congresses met. Franklin missed the First Continental Congress, but he was at the second.

democracy: a system of government in which power comes from the people. The people, in turn, allow their representatives to exercise this power for them. Britain had representatives, but the British king had the ultimate power.

Indian nation: native peoples who have formed a ruling group. In the 1600s and 1700s, the Indian nations of eastern North America included the Algonquians and the Lenape.

inoculate: to introduce a weakened form of a disease, such as smallpox, into someone's body so that the person becomes protected from getting it

Latin: the language spoken by the ancient Romans. In Franklin's time, it was still the language in which many scientific and philosophical works were written.

merchant trading: a business whose purpose is to exchange goods for money

paper money: paper notes issued to stand in for silver or gold coins. Recognized governments, such as the colony of New Jersey, were the only groups that could authorize the printing of money.

Pennsylvania proprietors: British king Charles II granted William Penn a tract of land in North America in 1681. The ruler, or proprietor, of this new colony—called Pennsylvania—would be William Penn and later on, his sons.

Puritans: a group of Protestant Christians who lived by a strict moral code. The group began in England in the 1500s, and many fled to America.

Quakers: also called the Society of Friends, a group of Protestant Christians that was founded in 1650. Quakers prefer simple religious services and are opposed to war.

revolt: a rebellion against a government

West Indies: a group of islands in the Caribbean Sea between the United States and South America

Source Notes

7 Esmond Wright, *Franklin of Philadelphia* (Cambridge, MA: Harvard University Press, 1986), 263.
7 Ibid., 270.
7 Ibid., 272.
16 Benjamin Franklin, *The Autobiography of Benjamin Franklin* (Reprint, Mineola, NY: Dover Publications, Inc., 1996), 15.
19 Ibid., 12.
21 Ibid., 16.
21 Ibid.
21 Ibid.
23 Ibid., 19.
25 Ibid., 21.
25 Ibid., 22.
25 Ibid.
26 Ibid., 26.
26 Ibid., 28.
26–27 Ibid.
27 Ibid., 30.
27 Ibid., 32.
28 Ibid.
30 Ibid., 52.
32 Ibid., 50.
32 Ibid., 85.
34 Ibid., 52.
36 Ibid., 53.
38 Benjamin Franklin [Richard Saunders, pseud.], *Poor Richard's Quotations, 1733 through 1758* (Boulder, CO: Blue Mountain Arts, 1975), 7, 8, 9, 20, 21, 23, 28, 32, 44, 48, 50, 76.
40 Franklin, 61.
41 Ibid., 79.
44 Wright, 58.
44 Franklin, 121.
47 Ibid.
51 Ronald W. Clark, *Benjamin Franklin: A New Biography* (New York: Random House, 1983), 144.
52 Ibid., 64.
52 H. W. Brands, *The First American: The Life and Times of Benjamin Franklin* (New York: Doubleday, 2000), 76.
55 Carl Van Doren, *Benjamin Franklin* (New York: Viking Penguin, 1991), 100.
55 Wright, 69.
61 Clark, 144.
63 Wright, 143.
64 Ibid.
68 Barbara Tuchman, *The March of Folly: From Troy to Vietnam* (New York: Ballantine Books, 1984), 165.
72 Clark, 230.
73 Catherine Drinker Bowen, *The Most Dangerous Man in America: Scenes from the Life of Benjamin Franklin* (Boston: Little, Brown, 1974), 231.
74 Wright, 227.
75 Ibid., 226.
76 Ibid., 232.
79–80 Ibid., 235.
93 Clark, 314.
99 Ibid., 288.
103 Wright, 343.
104 Ibid., 346.

SELECTED BIBLIOGRAPHY

"The Autobiography of Benjamin Franklin." *Archiving Early America.* n.d. <http://www.earlyamerica.com/lives/franklin/> (April 20, 2004).

"Benjamin Franklin: Glimpses of the Man." *The Franklin Institute Online.* 1994. <http://www.fi.edu/franklin/> (April 20, 2004).

Bowen, Catherine Drinker. *The Most Dangerous Man in America: Scenes from the Life of Benjamin Franklin.* Boston: Little, Brown, 1974.

Brands, H. W. *The First American: The Life and Times of Benjamin Franklin.* New York: Doubleday, 2000.

Clark, Ronald W. *Benjamin Franklin: A New Biography.* New York: Random House, 1983.

Franklin, Benjamin. "The Autobiography of Benjamin Franklin." *Project Gutenberg.* July 1994. <http://www.gutenberg.net/etext94/bfaut10.txt> (April 20, 2004).

Franklin, Benjamin. *Franklin: The Autobiography.* Edited and with an introduction by Daniel Aaron. Reprint, New York: Vintage Books, 1990.

Lopez, Claude-Ann. *Mon Cher Papa: Franklin and the Ladies of Paris.* New Haven, CT: Yale University Press, 1966.

Lopez, Claude-Ann, and Eugenia W. Herbert. *The Private Franklin: The Man and His Family.* New York: W. W. Norton & Company, Inc., 1975.

Tuchman, Barbara. *The March of Folly: From Troy to Vietnam.* New York: Ballantine Books, 1984.

Wright, Esmond. *Franklin of Philadelphia.* Cambridge, MA: Harvard University Press, 1986.

Further Reading and Websites

Ashby, Ruth. *The Amazing Mr. Franklin.* Atlanta: Peachtree Publishing, 2004.

"The Autobiography of Benjamin Franklin." *Archiving Early America.* n.d. <http://www.earlyamerica.com/lives/franklin/> (April 20, 2004).

"The Autobiography of Benjamin Franklin." *Project Gutenberg.* July 1994. <http://www.gutenberg.net/etext94/bfaut10.txt> (April 20, 2004).

"Benjamin Franklin: Glimpses of the Man." *The Franklin Institute Online.* 1994. <http://www.fi.edu/franklin/> (April 20, 2004).

Benjamin Franklin House. n.d. <http://www.rsa.org.uk/franklin/> (April 20, 2004).

Ben's Guide to U.S. Government for Kids. March 8, 2004. <http://bensguide.gpo.gov> (April 20, 2004).

Day, Nancy. *Your Travel Guide to Colonial America.* Minneapolis: Runestone Press, 2001.

Fleming, Candace. *Ben Franklin's Almanac: Being a True Account of the Good Gentleman's Life.* New York: Atheneum, 2003.

Giblin, James Cross. *The Amazing Life of Benjamin Franklin.* New York: Scholastic, 2000.

Gutman, Dan. *Qwerty Stevens Stuck in Time with Benjamin Franklin.* New York: Simon & Schuster, 2002.

Independence Hall Association. "The Electric Franklin." ushistory.org. 2004. <http://www.ushistory.org/franklin/> (April 20, 2004).

Noll, Cheryl Kirk. *The Ben Franklin Book of Easy and Incredible Experiments.* New York: John Wiley and Sons, 1995.

Schanzer, Rosalyn. *How Ben Franklin Stole the Lightning.* New York: HarperCollins, 2002.

INDEX

Adams, John, 7, 85, 88, 98
American Philosophical Society, 48–49
armonica, 62
Arnold, Benedict, 83–84

bifocals, 93
Boston, Massachusetts, 9, 10–11, 12, 13, 15, 16, 20, 21, 24–25, 43, 54, 68–71, 74, 77–78
Boston Tea Party, 74

colonists, 9, 33, 56, 58, 61, 65–72, 74, 77–84, 86–92, 97
Constitutional Convention, 101, 105
Continental Army, 84, 87, 95
Cushing, Thomas, 72

Deane, Silas, 89–90
Declaration of Independence, 85–86, 104
Declaratory Act, 68
Denham, Thomas, 28–30

Experiments and Observations on Electricity, 53

Franklin, Abiah Folger (mother), 10
Franklin, Benjamin: ambassador to France, 5–6, 90–99; apprentice to brother, 14–21; birth and childhood, 10–13; Constitutional Convention, 101–105; death, 104–105; Declaration of Independence committee, 85–86; deputy postmaster, 42–43, 64, 75; experiments with electricity, 5, 44–47, 52–55; inventions, 11, 45, 48, 54, 62, 93, 101, 105; marriage, 35–36; in the Pennsylvania Assembly, 56, 58, 63; running *The Pennsylvania Gazette*, 34, 42, 52; Second Continental Congress, 80–81, 83, 85–86, 88–90, 96, 99; writings, 15–16, 17–18, 19, 32, 34, 37–38, 41–42, 48, 50, 53, 67, 74, 104
Franklin, Deborah Read (wife), 23, 24, 26–28, 30, 34–36, 47, 59–60, 64, 67, 76
Franklin, Francis "Franky" (son), 36, 41
Franklin, James (brother), 14, 16–17, 18–21
Franklin, Josiah (father), 9–11, 12–14, 17, 20, 21, 26
Franklin, Sarah "Sally" (daughter), 47, 59, 60
Franklin, William (son), 35, 47–48, 55, 59, 62–63, 82, 100
Franklin, William Temple (grandson), 90
Franklin stove, 45
French and Indian War, 58

George III, 8, 80, 90

Homes, Robert, 24
Hutchinson, Thomas, 69, 71–75

Jefferson, Thomas, 85–86
"Join, or Die" cartoon, 56–57
Junto, 39, 104

Keimer, Samuel, 24–25, 30–31, 33–34
Keith, Sir William, 25–28

Lexington, Massachusetts, 78
Leyden jar experiment, 46

Library Company of
  Philadelphia, 39, 44
Lighthouse Tragedy, The, 15, 16
lightning rod, 54–55, 90
London, England, 26–28, 30, 43,
  59–60, 62, 64–67, 71, 73–74, 76
Louis XVI, 4–5, 8, 90

Meredith, Hugh, 31, 34
minuteman units, 78

New England Courant, 17, 18, 20

Parliament, 61, 65–68, 72, 75
Penn, Thomas, 43, 50–51, 60–61, 63
Penn, William, 43
Pennsylvania Assembly, 42, 44, 56, 58, 61, 63–64
Pennsylvania Gazette, The, 32–35, 42, 52
Philadelphia, Pennsylvania, 22, 25–32, 39–42, 44–45, 49–51, 59, 67, 79–81, 101, 105
Plain Truth, 50

Plan of Union, 56–57, 80
Poor Richard, 36–37
Poor Richard's Almanack, 37–38, 42, 52

redcoats, 70, 78, 95
Rutledge, Edward, 88

Second Continental Congress,
  80–83, 85–86, 88–90, 92, 96, 99
Sons of Liberty, 69, 71
Stamp Act, 64–68

Townshend duties, 69, 73
Treaty of Alliance, 96
Treaty of Amity and Commerce, 96

U.S. Constitution, 101, 103–104

Washington, George, 81, 87, 97
Whately, Thomas, 72–73

Yorktown, Virginia, 97

PHOTO ACKNOWLEDGMENTS

Photographs are used with the permission of: © CORBIS, p. 4; Library of Congress, pp. 6, 49, 51, 58, 85; © North Wind Picture Archives, pp. 9, 10, 15, 27, 29, 33, 36, 37, 45, 46, 66, 70, 78, 82, 91, 96, 102; © Hulton/Archive by Getty Images, pp. 13, 25, 31, 53, 60, 68, 75, 79, 97; © Bettmann/CORBIS, pp. 16, 40, 43, 55, 62, 93, 100; The Library Company of Philadelphia, pp. 18, 35; Independent Picture Service, pp. 22, 57; The White House Historical Association (White House Collection), p. 88.

Cover: Hulton/Archive by Getty Images